Original title:
Sharks in the Shadows

Copyright © 2025 Creative Arts Management OÜ
All rights reserved.

Author: Dexter Sullivan
ISBN HARDBACK: 978-1-80587-314-3
ISBN PAPERBACK: 978-1-80587-784-4

## Waves of Mystery

Beneath the foam, they joke and play,
With toothy grins, they swim all day.
Their friends are fish, with scales so bright,
They dance around, what a silly sight!

They peek out from the coral bed,
With secrets swimming in each head.
Not all are fierce, some giggle too,
And tickle the toes of divers' crew.

## Enigmatic Glides

Gliding past with a wink and a twist,
In a game of hide-and-seek, they insist.
The ocean's jesters, what are they up to?
Searching for snacks—or maybe a shoe?

A splash, a dive, then poof! They're gone,
Playing tag 'til the brightening dawn.
With bluster and cheer, they make their rounds,
In the deep blue where laughter resounds.

## **Underwater Watchers**

They peek from the rocks with a curious glance,
Missing one fin, have you seen their pants?
In currents chatty, like gossip they speak,
In bubbles of humor, their laughter's unique.

With eyes big and round, they spy on the fun,
At the coral disco, everyone's on the run.
With flips and swirls, they join the parade,
Who knew the briny depths could be this way made?

## The Depths' Embrace

In the gloomy waters, a ticklish spree,
With tickles and giggles, they're wild and free.
Their sharp little teeth can't hide their glee,
Swirling around on an underwater spree.

They whisper their tales to the bubbles above,
Of jellyfish waltzes and seawood love.
In their sneaky domain, they laugh and they twist,
Making the ocean a whimsical mist.

## The Depths' Dark Sentinels

In the blue where giggles play,
Those toothy grins come out to sway.
With sly smiles and fins so sleek,
They sneak a peek, just hide and seek.

Gliding softly through the sea,
What are they plotting? Come and see!
With a wiggle and a splashy spin,
They jest and jibe; watch out, my fin!

## Creatures of the Midnight Tide

Beneath the waves where shadows dance,
The mischief-makers prance and prance.
With beady eyes and silly quirks,
They steal the snacks that diver works.

Tickling clams and tapping shells,
They tell tall tales of ocean smells.
In midnight waters, laughter's ripe,
As they swap stories of their frightful hype.

## Watchers of the Forgotten Reef

Peeking out from coral crannies,
They play the role of ocean bunnies.
With silly flips and underwater dives,
They chase the fish that tease and connive.

Cogitating with a wink and grin,
Plotting how to join the din.
As seaweed sways and bubbles rise,
They form a band of fishy spies.

## Echoes from the Underworld

In deep blue realms where giggles echo,
The wise ones watch with scaly ghetto.
Their laughter bubbles up like foam,
As they conspire to bring us home.

In twilight zones, where secrets loom,
They orchestrate mischief in the gloom.
With a swish of tails and clever quips,
They embark on their stealthy trips.

## The Silent Thrum

In deep blue waves, they twirl and sway,
With toothy grins that chase clouds away.
They play a game, a hide-and-seek,
In tangled kelp, they're quite unique.

With bubbles blown, they laugh out loud,
Creating ripples, drawing a crowd.
Their fins like velvet, soft yet bold,
They dance, they glide, in stories untold.

## **Velvet Fins in the Moonlight**

With moonlit glimmers on slick and sleek,
They silently plot while we all sneak.
In sillier shapes, they dart and dive,
Who knew they had such jolly lives?

Their whispered giggles echo around,
As they prank the fish, always fooling the ground.
With a splash and a flip, they make their play,
While dreaming of snacks to brighten their day.

## The Hidden Realm's Guardians

In shadows they glide, in laughter they reign,
Protecting the seas, oh what a gain!
With curious eyes, they catch a glimpse,
Of fellow sea folk playing those limps.

With fins of silk, they guard the fun,
While plotting adventures under the sun.
Don't let their size give a shivery fright,
For they're the jokers of the deep night!

## Furtive Swimmers of the Twilight

In the twilight zone, they swing and sway,
With jolly hearts, they dance and play.
In stealthy stages, they leap with cheer,
The freshest of friends always near.

Their smiles are wide, their antics grand,
They send bubble letters with a flick of a fin hand.
As the sun dips low, with chuckles they roam,
Each wave is a song in their ocean home.

## Ocean's Midnight Watchers

In the moonlight's silvery gleam,
Creatures lurk, what a quirky theme.
They swim with grace, but hark, beware,
Jaws that giggle, a toothy flair.

With tiny jokes and playful flips,
Nameless prowlers making quips.
While fish all think they're safe and free,
It's just a midnight comedy.

## The Abyss's Watchful Gaze

Deep down where no one dares to peek,
A ticklish tickle gives a shriek.
Those staring eyes, all round and wide,
Like little jellybeans that glide.

With silly grins and cheeseball charms,
They swim along with goofy arms.
No threat in sight, just a funny scene,
The darkest depths hold laughter keen.

## Mysterious Currents

Waves that wiggle and swirl about,
Full of jokes, without a doubt.
The currents twist, with giggles they flow,
And bubble up with a silly show.

Fins that flounder, a wiggly dance,
They're on the lookout for a chance.
To surprise the sun, with splashes and glints,
While all the mermaids roll in hints.

## Elegance of the Silent Chomp

Floating gently on silent thrones,
They smirk with teeth, like little loans.
A dash of grace, with puny bites,
Those armored knights, in the moonlit nights.

In velvety waters, they plot and scheme,
Dream up a feast, or a cartoon dream.
But those that linger, sure of their fate,
Will find themselves in a giggling slate.

## Lurkers of the Midnight Tide

In murky waters, there's a team,
With fins that glide, they make a dream.
They sneak and peek with toothy grins,
In the great blue sea, they love to spin.

When night falls down, they love to play,
With friends and fish, they'll sway and sway.
A tickle here, a splash of fun,
They're up to mischief 'til the rising sun.

## Guardians of the Ocean Depths

From crevices deep, they watch and wait,
With eyes so wide, they contemplate.
A game of peek-a-boo, oh so sly,
With teeth like forks and a curious eye.

At crunch time, they crack jokes galore,
As sea turtles giggle and dolphins roar.
They guard the seas with a comical twist,
In the balmy waves, who can resist?

## Dancers of the Depths

Underneath the waves, they take a chance,
With a wiggly tail, they start to dance.
Round and round in a watery whirl,
They twirl and giggle, giving a twirl.

With jellyfish partners, they sway with glee,
In a grand ballet, oh come and see!
An ocean floor stage, where fun's the key,
With fin and flair, they're wild and free.

## Beneath the Surface

Down where the bubbles float and pop,
A giggling gang decides to stop.
They throw a party beneath the foam,
Each wave a discord, it feels like home.

With crabby snacks and seaweed cake,
They laugh and sing for the ocean's sake.
A finny fiesta, such joyous charms,
In the silent depths, they'll raise alarms!

## **Secrets in the Dark Waters**

Beneath the waves they glide with glee,
A toothy grin for you and me.
With sleek moves, they dance and twist,
Whispers of tales that none could list.

In the murky depths, they play a game,
Hide and seek, never the same.
Bubble blowing, a frothy roar,
Caught in antics, oh what a chore!

Invisible fins in the moonlit glow,
Sneaky giggles, below they flow.
Living legends, with mischief stored,
Jokes on land, they can't afford!

So if you swim where secrets thrive,
Beware the smiles that come alive.
For in the depths, with laughter bright,
The jesters wait to give a fright!

## **Veiled Intentions**

In the depths, where shadows roam,
They've planned a party, far from home.
Clowning around with a splashy flair,
Dressed in stripes for a midnight affair.

With keen senses and eyes so wide,
They plot the pranks, with friends beside.
Toothsome chuckles on the breeze,
Their shenanigans aim to tease.

Wiggly tails and giggles galore,
Splashback games that shake the shore.
They hide behind rocks, just for fun,
Chasing moonbeams, oh what a run!

So if you find a bubble trail,
It's just a sign to follow their tale.
For under the waves, in secret schemes,
Are creatures bound by laughter and dreams!

**Tides of the Unknown**

Under the surface, where currents flow,
Witty whispers paint the show.
They glide through ripples, light as air,
Giggling ghouls, with sand in their hair.

In the dip and dive of the tide, so free,
Chasing each other like kids at spree.
Fins in concert, a slippery ballet,
Each flip and twist leads the way to play.

With shadows prancing, they roam with flair,
Their little tricks dance everywhere.
In this watery world, bizarre and grand,
They jest and jive, a playful band!

So if you hear a splash and snicker,
Don't be fooled, it's just their trickster.
For in the depths, a jovial crew,
Stirs up delight for me and you!

## Wanderers of the Midnight Sea

Through the swells, with a flip and whirl,
They twist and turn in a silvery swirl.
As midnight travelers, bold and spry,
Under the stars, they leap and fly.

With a wink and nod, they slip away,
Casting shadows in the foam's ballet.
Fins like saucers, round and bright,
Crafting giggles in the pale moonlight.

Oh what a laugh, in frothy swells,
With stories of secrets no one tells.
Adventurers bold, on mischief bent,
Creating ripples with good intent!

So if you venture where the moonbeams gleam,
Find joy in shadows, live the dream.
Wanderers beneath the celestial spree,
Bubbling with laughter, a sight to see!

## Beneath Nature's Surface

In the depths, they wiggle with glee,
Making fishy friends for tea.
With toothy grins, they do a dance,
Inviting all for a cheeky prance.

They play hide and seek in the coral maze,
With silly flips, they love to amaze.
As bubbles rise and laughter flows,
Underwater giggles, where nobody knows.

Silly fins and wiggly tails,
Chasing shadows like playful snails.
Their humor sparkles like light on waves,
Nature's jesters, oh how they behave!

So when you swim near the ocean's floor,
Look for the jokes and seek out more.
With a splash and a laugh, they keep it bright,
Making the deep a hilarious sight!

## Ocean's Chameleons

Colorful jesters in a watery glow,
Painting the sea, putting on a show.
With scales that shimmer and change with flair,
They giggle and wiggle without a care.

Hiding in reefs, playing the fool,
Turning the tide of the ocean's school.
With a wink and a nudge, they swim with style,
Cracking up waves, making it worthwhile.

In the currents of blue, they craft a jest,
Floating like fluff, they simply know best.
Masters of disguise, they don't take a dive,
Joking and jiving, they keep the vibe alive.

So join in their frolic, don't hesitate,
In the dance of the deep, you might find your fate.
With laughter and splashes, they rule the sea,
Sea's chameleons, oh what joy to see!

## **The Currents' Secret Keepers**

Whispers and giggles swirl in the tide,
Where playful creatures love to hide.
With wiggles and bubbles, they share a grin,
The secrets they hold? Let the fun begin!

In the eddies, they tell silly tales,
While chasing each other with flicks of their tails.
From shells to seaweed, they weave a plot,
Of how one lost a shoe, and the other forgot.

Darting about like a rollercoaster,
With chuckles and splashes, a real creek poster.
The current laughs as it flows along,
Keeping the fun in its bubbly song.

Join the party, dive in with glee,
In the currents' arms, let yourself be free.
The hidden jesters make stories unfold,
In the watery depths, where laughter is gold!

**Elusive Sculptors of the Deep**

Crafting a ballet with fins and tails,
Sculptors of mischief in underwater trails.
With a flick of a flipper, they shape the fun,
Creating ocean art, second to none.

In sandy galleries, they hold a spree,
Drawing smiles with every splash and glee.
Their masterpieces twirl in a watery dance,
Elusive artists, giving joy a chance.

From the shadows they pop, just for a laugh,
Sketching the sea in a whimsical path.
With tickles of light, they bring out the cheer,
Making memories in depths so clear.

So cherish the laughter found in the blue,
Where sculptors of joy are waiting for you.
With each hidden wave, let your spirit leap,
For the treasures they hold are secrets to keep!

**Dance of the Abyssal Beasts**

In waters deep where giggles hide,
A creature twirls, with fins so wide.
It spins around, a giddy sight,
In darkness damp, it dances light.

With tiny teeth and goofy grin,
It leaps for joy, a playful fin.
Bubbles burst as laughter swells,
These clumsy beasts hide secret spells.

They glide and flop, a sight to see,
In depths of blue, they love to flee.
Chasing snacks with silly glee,
These quirky friends are wild and free.

So if you glance beneath the waves,
Watch for the antics of these knaves.
A splash, a swirl, a joyful tease,
In the deep sea, there's no unease!

## Gliding Through the Darkness

In murky depths where few dare roam,
A glider slips, far from its home.
With flappy fins it starts to prance,
Beneath the waves, it loves to dance.

Its buddy's eyes are big and round,
A sassy tail flutters, oh, what a sound!
Around the rocks, they sneak and peek,
In midnight fun, they play hide and seek.

They flip and flop with cheeky flair,
In the deep sea's chilly air.
Each twist and turn brings laughter dear,
As they glide past, they bring good cheer.

So if you're swimming near the blue,
Keep an eye out, you might just view,
These merry misfits with a grin,
Floating along, let the fun begin!

## Night's Unseen Guardians

At night when waves are cold and brash,
Two buddies roam with a comical splash.
They guard the depths with silly poses,
In the dark, they strike playful dozes.

With toothy grins that never fade,
They chuckle softly, a finned parade.
They keep the secrets of the tide,
With goofy pouts, they swell with pride.

In shadows deep, they twist and spin,
Showing off their fins with cheeky grin.
Each bubble bursts with a joyous sound,
As they frolic and dance around.

So venture forth with a heart so light,
In the underwater world, pure delight.
For in the night, when all seems grim,
These unseen guardians will make you swim!

## The Moonlit Predator's Dance

Under the shine of the silver moon,
A creature moves to an odd little tune.
With googly eyes and a wobbly glide,
It's a dance of mischief from side to side.

It sways through coral, a circus show,
With pirouettes, it puts on a glow.
In the shadows, laughter brightens the night,
As the sneaky beast emerges in sight.

Let's not forget its clumsy friends,
Joining in where the laughter blends.
With each turn, they add to the cheer,
In the moonlit ball that brings them near.

So watch and laugh as they take the stage,
In this watery world, there's little rage.
For in the depths, where the funny prance,
The joy of the night is an epic dance!

## The Ocean's Cloaked Symphony

In the deep where bubbles play,
Fins sneak past like folks in gray.
They dance in currents, quite a sight,
While seaweed giggles, soft and light.

With a wiggle and a splash so grand,
They sneak around, a quirky band.
Bubbles burst in laughter's tune,
As fishy pranks happen 'neath the moon.

A fin pokes out, then hides away,
Making crabs jump and fish delay.
Every nudge becomes a race,
Undersea, it's a silly place.

When a giant bubble pops with glee,
It startles every fish and bee.
In a world where antics rule,
The ocean sings; it's one big pool.

**Sins of the Deep Currents**

Whispers swirl beneath the foam,
Guilty fins begin to roam.
Each nibble and each cheeky grin,
Secrets wrapped in algae thin.

A clam with pearls shakes its shell,
Claiming that it knows too well.
But every creature plays its part,
In this underwater art.

A stinky sock from shore comes by,
Causing fish to gasp and sigh.
"Who left this here?" they swim and peep,
As laughter echoes from the deep.

Even an octopus can trip,
On jellies' pranks, they take a dip.
Sins of the currents, none can hide,
Undersea giggles, a joy-filled ride.

## The Undersea Conundrum

With a wink and a flick of the tail,
Bubbles rise like a giddy hail.
A question circles in the tide,
"Who's playing hide-and-seek?" they cried.

A dolphin laughs, flipping real high,
"Catch me if you can!" it'll sly.
The fish all dart, a comical chase,
In the twisted sea, it's a racy space.

A clam and crab do a silly jig,
While squids get tangled, oh so big.
"What's a conundrum?" asks the pouty ray,
"It's finding fun in every sway!"

As currents swirl and laughter rings,
In the depths where the sea life sings.
Joyful trails of frolic dive,
In this ocean, who's really alive?

## Veil of the Ocean's Giants

Beneath the waves, where laughter hides,
Creatures dance, in fishy rides.
With toothy grins, they play their games,
Chasing bubbles, forgetting names.

In stealthy gowns of seawater blue,
They twirl and twist, a comical crew.
With goofy flips and silly spins,
In their world, everyone wins.

Each peep from below stirs a smile,
As they navigate the ocean's aisle.
With stern faces that can't disguise,
Witty woes and fishy lies.

They poke their fins, just for a laugh,
Tickling friends, like a playful gaff.
In this grand stage of watery fun,
Life's a joke, they've already won!

## Sinews of the Abyss

In twilight depths, with giggles abound,
Creatures frolic without a sound.
With tangled limbs and jiggly flair,
They throw a party, underwater fair.

They juggle shells and wiggle with glee,
Using seaweed as their marquee.
With spiraled heads and silly trails,
They dance in rhythm, dodging snails.

Fins flap wildly, like sails in a breeze,
Unfurling wonders with grand expertise.
Beneath the surface, join the fun,
In the dark, the laughter's never done.

Don't forget the tales they weave,
With puns and jests, it's hard to believe.
Sinewy friends in deep, dark hoods,
Turn oceanic gloom into neighborhoods!

## Fins of the Forgotten Realm

In realms unseen, where legends play,
Witty fish splash in a cabaret.
With fins that flutter and giggles that soar,
They'll keep you laughing, wanting more.

With a wink and a twist, they glide through the mist,
In a world where serious can't coexist.
Chasing the drift of forgotten dreams,
Turning the tide with their charming schemes.

In hidden caverns, they weave their tales,
Of floating treasures and cryptic gales.
With every flip, a comet prevails,
Tickling the sea with soggy details.

So join the fun on this bizarre ride,
In gurgling laughter, let worries slide.
For here in this realm, the playful reign,
And every fin tells of joy and pain!

## Shadows of the Deep Blue

In murky corners, mischief brews,
Creatures giggle in vibrant hues.
Hiding in kelp, their antics unfold,
With tales of bravado that never gets old.

Tiny minions in a sprawling spree,
Plotting adventures, as silly as can be.
They play peek-a-boo with crabs and snails,
Using shadows to tell vibrant tales.

With caution thrown to the bubbling foam,
In those dark depths, they call it home.
Acrobatics abound, flips and swirls,
Their laughter bubbles like pearls unfurl.

From gloomy depths, joy brightly beams,
As laughter mingles with watery dreams.
So come and see, if you dare,
The shenanigans, you'll find everywhere!

## Midnight's Veil

In the ocean's cloak so dark,
A toothy grin leaves quite a mark.
With fins that flicker in the night,
They dance like ghouls, a spooky sight.

They sport a wink and playful flair,
As bubbles burst and fill the air.
A comet's tail, they glide and swoop,
In this grand underwater loop.

Giggles echo in the brine,
As shadows tease the waves divine.
With every splash and every cheer,
They chase the dolphins like a sphere.

Who knew the night could be so rad?
These ocean tricks aren't just a fad.
With cartwheels as the moonlight glows,
They flaunt a charm that only flows.

**Eclipsed by the Ocean Depths**

Underneath the frothy waves,
A mystery's making laughter behave.
With giant grins and giggles grand,
They plan a party on the sand.

A bubble's pop draws all their eyes,
As pranks unfold beneath the skies.
With seaweed wigs and silly dance,
They swirl and twirl — a comical chance.

A tangle here, a fin that trips,
Creating chaos in quick quips.
With every twist, a chuckle rings,
In depths where laughter takes to wings.

Eclipsed by bubbles, they unite,
In moonlit mischief, pure delight.
Those playful swirls beneath the tide,
A wonder where goldfish take a ride.

## Luminous Sentries of the Sea

In the depths where lanterns glow,
With playful jests, they steal the show.
Shimmering scales of every hue,
Creating mischief in the blue.

A flick and swish, a chortle bright,
Hiding treasures out of sight.
With every giggle, nets are cast,
In ocean games, oh what a blast!

When darkness falls, they steal the dance,
Inviting all to join the chance.
With silly tricks that catch the eye,
And wink as bubbles drift on by.

Luminous jesters, bold and spry,
With jokes that float and never die.
As waves carry their laughter far,
They revel under the shining star.

## The Enigmatic Silence

In quiet depths where secrets roam,
The giddiest jesters find a home.
In mystery's glare, a grin awakes,
As shadows slip and a giggle breaks.

What's lurking here in playful hues?
A hint of trouble, some ocean clues.
They snicker low at the bubble's jest,
In silliness, they are truly blessed.

When silence reigns, their antics bloom,
They craft their laughter, filling room.
A tickle in the water's weave,
That's the spell of what they leave.

With every drip, a ripple spreads,
As they spin tales in ocean threads.
In shadows cast by moonlit charms,
The giggles hide in the watery arms.

## **Entwined with the Abyss**

In murky depths where giggles dwell,
Swirling fins cast quite the spell.
A dance of jaws, a cheeky grin,
For every fish that's lost its kin.

With wiggly wiggles and flip-flop tails,
The ocean's court brings merry tales.
In swirling pools, they leap and glide,
A wobbly laugh, no place to hide.

With bubbles rising, they speak in glee,
Reeling in pranks like it's a spree.
Twisting about in playful glee,
Who knew the deep could cause such glee?

So forget your worries and take a dive,
In the depths, the chuckles thrive.
For every splash, a joke on tap,
In the abyss, there's no mishap.

## **Veiled Masters of Might**

With stealth, they glide, the jesters bold,
In cloaks of water, their laughter told.
With toothy smiles, they take the stage,
Masters of comedy, complete with rage.

Behind the veils where shadows play,
They prank the currents, night and day.
Making fish jump with a surprising bite,
In the moonlit dance, it's quite the sight.

Grand comedians with paddles to steer,
They weave through depths where giggles sneer.
Each twist and turn a humorous feat,
In nature's theater, they're hard to beat.

Hilarity reigns in waters deep,
Where laughter echoes and secrets creep.
From reef to rock, their antics flow,
In the dark, they put on a show.

## Nomads of the Abyss

Wandering depths with curious flair,
On aquatic highways, they dance without care.
Nimble and sneaky, they glide with ease,
A prankster squad in a swirling breeze.

With fins like sails, they roam the blue,
Covering ground, just like a crew.
Tickling the currents, they flip and twine,
In laughter's embrace, they feel divine.

Grinning at dusk, with a wink and a sway,
The night adorns them in frolicsome play.
Amongst the fray, their laughter rings,
Glorious mischief, the joy it brings!

In an endless ocean, they seek and jest,
Chasing tales, they know it best.
For every swim is a tale complete,
In nomad's quest, they can't be beat.

## In the Gloom of the Aquatic Night

In moonlit gleams where secrets thrive,
They twirl and twist, a comical drive.
With eyes aglow, they scheme and plot,
Underwater antics that hit the spot.

Every ripple holds a joke or two,
Swimming through shadows, they share their view.
Lurking behind rocks, with a mischievous grin,
Each playful splash whispers, "Let's begin!"

In the darkest depths, chuckles unfold,
A comedy show, forever bold.
Their underwater circus is truly grand,
With laughter resounding across the sand.

So when the sun sets and the shadows creep,
Join the giggles that rise from the deep.
In aquatic nights where jesters dwell,
Good vibes spread like a sea shanty bell.

## The Siren's Mirage

In waters deep, they prance and play,
With toothy smiles, they glide away.
They chase the fish, oh what a sight,
In swirling dance, they're full of fright.

Fins like blades, they twirl with glee,
Pretending to be as cute as can be.
But when they yawn, it's quite a show,
Just watch your toes, or off they'll go!

## Fanged Specters of the Sea

In the murky depths, they joke and jive,
With gnashing teeth, they feel alive.
They wink and nod, in hopes you see,
Their big grins hiding a comedy spree!

With every splash, there's giggles loud,
As they flub around, so suave and proud.
They're out for laughs, not meant to scare,
Just check your ankles, or do beware!

## The Quiet Architects of the Abyss

Building castles from the sand,
With toothy grins and steady hands.
They take their time, so structured and neat,
While pretending it's all a fun little feat.

They'll show you plans, all drawn askew,
And laugh aloud like it's brand new.
But next you know, there's a silly clash,
Their dreams of grandeur just turned to ash!

## **Fluid Whispers Beneath**

In silent jokes, they swim around,
With swishes here and laughter sound.
They plot and scheme with giggle fits,
A dance of fin, the ocean's wits.

Their whispers drift on tides so high,
As bubbles rise, and jokes comply.
Just keep it light, right in their game,
Or you'll be part of their silly fame!

**Abyssal Sentinels**

In twilight's grip, where fish do dart,
A fin appears, an artful part.
They plot and cheer in ocean's dance,
With toothy grins, they take their chance.

With every splash, the laughter's near,
A bubble emerges, quick as fear.
In silent woods, they play their game,
A jest that flares, ignites the same.

The glimmering scales, a laughing bunch,
At lunch they gather, munch and crunch.
Like comedians dressed in fin-lined suits,
They twist and tumble, never brutes.

So if you hear a giggle soft,
It's just the finned who play aloft.
Wily jesters in the wet abyss,
Their merry antics we will miss.

## **Whispers of the Coastal Depths**

Beneath the waves, where bubbles rise,
A glee of grins and playful sighs.
With sneaky moves, they do confide,
In currents fast, they start to glide.

They tell tall tales of tasty feasts,
A party here, with all the least.
With winks and flicks, they dart with style,
Each flip a giggle, a toothy smile.

On sandy shores where surfers peek,
They joke and jibe, oh what a squeak!
The sun shines down, they swim with flair,
Making merry in the salty air.

So listen close to ocean's jest,
In deep blue realms, they find their best.
With every splash, a chuckle grows,
In silent depth where friendship flows.

## Crouching Waves

In the swell where shadows play,
Figures loom in a funny way.
They hide and sneak, a playful crew,
Crafty moves as the tide flows through.

Low and slow, they wriggle deep,
Mischief made while fishy sleep.
With splash and splash, they hoot in glee,
A cupping wave, my oh my me!

Wrapped in kelp, they wait in line,
With two big eyes, oh how they shine!
Atop a rock, a jester lays,
A comedy show in sea's ballets.

Though fierce their bite might seem to boast,
In hidden shrouds, they love the most.
The water's pranksters, let it be known,
With every wave, their laughter's grown.

## Teeth Beneath the Tranquil Surface

Beneath the calm, a giggle blooms,
Where dark hues swim in hidden rooms.
With shiny teeth that catch the light,
They plan their tricks from morn to night.

Like puppets made of fin and scale,
They sneak around without a trail.
A flash, a whirl, a race begins,
With every twist, the ocean grins.

In the deep, they spin and dive,
Where feeble fish seem not to thrive.
For every act, there's playful cheer,
With friendly bites, they persevere.

So when you ponder deep blue fears,
Remember laughter, not just tears.
In gleeful depths, with fins that sway,
They're just the jesters of the bay.

## **Ocean's Choreography**

In the water, they twist and twirl,
With fins like dancers, giving a whirl.
They sneak up close, then dart away,
It's a game of tag at the break of day.

Their grins are wide, with a toothy show,
Chasing fish, in a wiggly flow.
While bubbles pop, and currents sway,
These underwater jesters join the ballet.

In the reefs, they strut and glide,
With secret moves, in the blue they hide.
Yet all the while, there's mischief around,
As ocean's stars do pirouettes profound.

So here they come, with a splash and a laugh,
Masters of the deep, diving their craft.
They leap and frolic, totally unplanned,
Teaching us all, how to live unscanned.

## Echoes of the Deep Hunter

Echoes ripple through the vast blue sea,
Where jesters reside, wild and free.
Hiding tight, behind great rocks,
Daring each other to knock off their socks.

With a flick of their tails, they play their tricks,
Masters of stealth, in playful flicks.
Glancing at schools, they share a grin,
'Let's give them a show, and watch them spin!'

They're like underwater pranksters gone mad,
Doing silly flips that make you glad.
They chuckle and gurgle, beneath the foam,
Oh, what a performance under the comb!

So heed the rumble, the echoes near,
A comedy show that brings us cheer.
Nature's jesters in a brilliant surround,
With laughter and bubbles where fun can be found.

## **Furtive Glimmers of the Tide**

In twilight hues, they bask and peek,
With sneaky smiles, they play hide and seek.
Glimmering eyes in the fading light,
A comedy cast for the coming night.

Witty whispers ripple through their realm,
As shadows glide like a quirky helm.
They flounder about, in a silvery glow,
Sharing secrets only the waves would know.

With a splashy joke, they sneak and dive,
Crafting capers that keep them alive.
Their antics cause a ruckus so grand,
A timeless sketch in this watery land.

So laugh along with the tides' sweet jest,
Join in their play; it's what they do best.
Under the moonlight, the fun won't subside,
In the playful abyss where these glimmers glide.

## **Predatory Shadows at Dusk**

As the sun sinks low, the games begin,
Underneath the waves, they sport a fin.
With sly little giggles, they start to plot,
A shadowy caper, connecting each dot.

They glide oh-so-smooth, like a stealthy ace,
In search of a laugh, while keeping their pace.
One nudges the other, 'Time for some fun!'
The night is young; let's see who will run!

With a flick of the fin and a wink of the eye,
A comedic chase as they all dart by.
In a world of mischief, it's hard to tell
Where endearing chuckles and antics dwell.

So as night approaches, don't forget to look,
For playful prowlers, in this watery nook.
Their shadows will dance, in a ridiculous play,
Laughing at twilight as they fade away.

## A Dance with the Abyss

In the depths where giggles play,
Fish wear hats for a grand ballet,
With twirls and twists in seaweed skirts,
They dance around while the ocean smirks.

A tickle from a fin, a bubble burst,
They whirl and spin, a giggly thirst,
The moonlight winks at this quirky sight,
As sea critters frolic in the night.

With jellyfish in jeans and crabs in shoes,
They throw a party with ocean blues,
Chasing shadows beneath the waves,
Where silliness thrives and laughter saves.

Together they sway, the ocean's jest,
In this watery world, they laugh the best,
So if you peek where the ripples sway,
You might join in their dance someday!

## Undercurrents of the Unknown

Bubbles rise with a squeaky sound,
What mischief lurks where no one's found?
A burp from a fish, a jellyfish sigh,
Who knew sea secrets made us cry?

With googly eyes and noses that squeak,
The ocean's creatures love to peek,
Under rocks and the swirling brine,
Beneath the waves, it's humor divine.

Octopus in tux, looking quite dapper,
While clams gossip in a bubble trapper,
Turtles wearing hats made of sea foam,
Who knew the beach could feel like home?

So if you float where the tides collide,
Listen closely, enjoy the ride,
For laughter echoes in every wave,
In the depths where the playful creatures misbehave!

## The Silent Loom

In the quiet depths where shadows creep,
A weaving tale for the brave to keep,
An angler in a hat, casting a line,
Sparks giggles from fish with cheeks so fine.

Threads of laughter, woven with glee,
As ghostly shapes dance, wild and free,
The crabs tell secrets, while the rays wiggle,
In a magical loom, the bubbles giggle.

A seahorse in slippers prances on by,
While sea cucumbers chew on a pie,
There's mischief afoot in this tranquil scene,
Where the waves and whispers weave so keen.

As currents hum songs of silly zest,
Life beneath flows with joyous jest,
Dive deep enough and you'll surely see,
The humor spun in deep mystery!

## Fluid Shadows Beneath

Waves roll in with a slappy tap,
Where the fishy crew takes a silly nap,
A turtle snores, a clam gives a snort,
Underwater dreams at their favorite port.

A plankton parade with a comical cheer,
As tiny critters waltz, drawing all near,
The anchors play tag and the seashells blare,
Under the foam, fun is found everywhere.

Ghostly figures flick and dive,
In fluid mischief, they come alive,
A dolphin winks as he shows off his flip,
While bubbles play tricks, a slippery trip.

So next time you glance at the ocean's face,
Remember its tales of jolly grace,
For in those depths, laughter takes flight,
In fluid shadows, joy shines bright!

**Teeth that Glint like Stars**

In the ocean, smiles so wide,
Bright and shiny, what a ride!
They're not to eat your lunch, you see,
Just shining bright, like glee on spree.

With a chuckle and a twist of fate,
Those pearly whites just love to prate.
Hey buddy, can I borrow a snack?
No worries, friend, I won't bite back!

Fishing lines and seaweed fun,
Tooth fairy's swim just begun.
Watch them glide with all their flair,
In their shiny teeth, we'll share a glare.

So if you swim in ocean's play,
Just remember, it's a toothy day!
Laugh with them, just give a shout,
And don't you dare make them pout!

## **Lurkers in the Blackened Reef**

Beneath the waves, a playful tease,
For creatures lurking with such ease.
Are they friends or just a jest?
You'll laugh and scream; it's quite the quest!

With fins a-flip and tails a-swish,
They pop up quick—oh, what a dish!
They hide behind a coral throne,
Saying, 'Come play! We're not alone!'

Just peek-a-boo from darkened spots,
Oh look, they've found your lunch; oh, knots!
In the depths, they take their stance,
Waiting for you—let's do a dance!

So next time you're wading near the blue,
Be ready for friends who love a view.
Laughter bubbles, it's the norm,
In the reef where giggles form!

## The Enigma of the Deep Blue

What's hiding under waves so deep?
A riddle wrapped, a secret keep.
It tickles fins with a coy embrace,
Come find the fun in this weird place!

With poky teeth like little spikes,
They giggle softly, oh what hikes!
A mystery shrouded, yet so bright,
Who knew the deep could bring such light?

Finding seashells, what a feat!
They whisper, 'Dance, don't miss a beat!'
In currents swift, they twirl and glide,
Let's join the fun, just hop inside!

So swim along with joyful cheer,
Those playful souls are always near.
In deep blue depths, the laughter's found,
A giggle fest in watery ground!

## Veils of Water and Mystery

Through veils of water, a tale unfolds,
With creatures grinning, oh so bold.
Each ripple brings a joke to share,
In watery lanes, they dance and flare.

Behind the bubbles, a sight to see,
Glinting eyes, full of glee!
They lurk and joke, just out of sight,
Winking at you, what a delight!

With splashes bright and giggles round,
What mischief in the sea can be found!
Join their games with joyous might,
And swim away till the day turns night.

So if you ever feel the pull,
Of whims and wonders, playful and full,
Dive right in, let laughter flow,
In veils of water, fun will grow!

## Cruelty in the Calm

In the depths where giggles hide,
A toothy grin does glide.
With a flick of their tail, they plot,
Tasty snacks on the menu, for a whole lot!

In laughter's grasp, they play the game,
Chasing bubbles, but who's to blame?
"Watch your toes!" they cry with glee,
As they whirl around, like a wild spree!

Bubbles burst with silly sounds,
These ocean jesters spin 'round and 'round.
But beware the playful bite,
Not a meal, just a laugh in the night!

In the tranquil sea, pranks unfold,
With a nibble or two, their mischief is gold.
For in calm waters, jesters dwell,
In a game of laugh and a bite as well!

## Pirates of the Dark Current

In murky depths where shadows dart,
Pirate teeth with a devious art!
They sail the current, masks of glee,
With a treasure chest of giggles, just wait and see!

With an eye patch on, they hide and seek,
"Arrr, we'll have fun until you squeak!"
A flip of the fin, a splash of delight,
Pirating laughs, they rule the night!

With each wave, a hearty cheer,
The undersea bandits draw near!
"Keep your limbs close, it's all in jest,
We're just playing, no need to stress!"

In the dark, they plot and sneak,
A treasure map made of laughter, unique!
So join the crew of giggles and fun,
In this watery tale, we're never done!

## **Silent Hunters Beneath the Waves**

Beneath calm tides, they flit and glide,
Silent prowlers with a wink of pride.
With a giggle and twist, they swoosh,
In a stealthy race, they squash and swoosh!

With stealth of legend, they take their time,
Sneaking up with a fishy rhyme.
"Surprise!" they yell with toothy cheer,
In games of hide, they appear, disappear!

At twilight's kiss, they prance and play,
Hiding in the shadows, hip-hip hooray!
In this underwater game of tag,
Laughter echoes, and they wag!

With fins a-flap and smiles wide,
These hunters glide with playful pride.
In depths unknown, where fun resides,
They swim along with friendly strides!

## Predators of the Deep

In ocean's cradle, they laugh out loud,
Predators cloaked in playful shroud.
With massive jaws and hearty grins,
They munch on seaweed, where the fun begins!

"Why the long face?" they tease and taunt,
In the dining hall, it's always a jaunt.
With a flick of a fin and a whirl around,
Giggles ripple, and joy abounds!

With a splish and splash, they charge along,
Singing silly tunes, a merry throng.
"Careful now, keep your limbs on tight,
We eat in jest, without a fright!"

In the depths, where hilarity meets,
Predators twirl to their own beats.
Beneath the waves, where humor flows,
The ocean's jesters steal the shows!

## **Peril in the Dark Foam**

Underneath the murky wave,
Something wiggles, misbehaves.
Is it a fish or kind of junk?
That tickles toes and gives a funk?

With big teeth grinning, quite absurd,
They plot to steal your sandwich, blurred.
A flip and splash, a laugh so loud,
Is that a shark or just a crowd?

Watch your toes when you take a dip,
They paddle near; it's a stealthy trip.
But don't be scared, they just want fun,
In soggy capers, we all run.

Forget the bite, they crave a pet,
Swim with them, you won't regret.
Just bring some snacks, and you will see,
These dark foam dwellers dance with glee.

## **Blue Depths Conceal**

In the ocean, wrap and weave,
All the fishy tricks, believe.
Bubbles pop, a giggle floats,
Something's lurking near the moats.

Swirling through the deep blue veil,
What's that bump? A silly tail!
It's not a menace, just a tease,
A little prankster, at its ease.

The creatures flash, a gleeful sight,
In near-darkness, they play at night.
Chasing tides, they spin and twirl,
Ahoy! A fin, a whirl and swirl!

With cheeky grins, they dance about,
Who knew the depths could bring a shout?
This harmless charm in waves so blue,
Is just a party meant for you!

## Specters of the Open Ocean

In shadows cast by glittered sheen,
A wobbly dance, what a scene!
Nimble fins, a playful jest,
These ocean phantoms know best.

They slide through water, handsome foes,
With playful smiles that nobody knows.
A fin that pokes, a bubble burst,
In jolly mischief, they will thirst.

They race and splash, in beams of sun,
"Catch me if you can!", is their fun.
With finned antics, they take the stage,
The ocean floor turns into a cage!

The nimble games, they raucous cheer,
So grab your float, and bring your gear.
For in this realm of watery lore,
The specters play forevermore.

## Beneath the Surface's Veil

Beneath the waves, where secrets twine,
A comical world, truly divine.
Jellyfish jiving, in crazy dress,
The underwater ball—no need to impress!

With swirling tails and silly pranks,
These cheeky dancers steal our thanks.
A curtain lift; what's that I see?
A giddy grin, come join the spree!

"Don't bite, just tickle!" they chant aloud,
Their laughter echoes, draws a crowd.
Swim side by side, flippers in tow,
Let's dance to the beat of joyful flow!

With every splash, a giggle bursts,
Their underwater charms, a belly-to-chest.
So come on down, grab a friend,
In the depths of laughter, the fun won't end!

## Glimmers in the Gloom

In the deep where the giggles hum,
Fish tell tales of a finned old chum.
With a grin that could scare,
But he just wants to share a rare sea pear.

He glides with grace, a curious sight,
Sipping bubbles while dodging light.
Munching on kelp, so nonchalant,
While schools of fish just laugh and flaunt.

A comic in fins, he's got tricks galore,
Performs for crabs on the ocean floor.
No fright in sight, just the splashes and twirls,
As lobsters cheer for the finned goofball curls.

From gloom to giggles, joy finds its way,
Beneath the waves where the jesters play.
With a flip of his tail, the laughter will spread,
In the depths of the sea where all worries are shed.

## Ocean's Whispered Secrets

Beneath the swell, a whispering grazes,
Of mischief and munch in the tide's thick mazes.
Chuckles echo as bubbles leap,
In this underworld where secrets creep.

A toothy grin says, "Wanna play tag?"
But he's just a softy, not one to brag.
With laughter like pearls, he glimmers with glee,
While tickling the fins of a passing sea bee.

With sprightly dashes, he zooms to impress,
While octopuses giggle in their own little dress.
Tales of the deep come with jokes on the scale,
Where each sandy shenanigan tells a tale.

Oh, what a ruckus beneath the blue is made,
In the ocean's embrace, no worries invade.
Light-hearted frolickers dance in the sea,
As laughter's the currency of blissful decree.

## Jaws Beneath the Surface

In the dark where the currents spin,
A toothy grin peeks with a cheeky grin.
He swirls through the waves, a playful ghost,
Dancing with seaweed, he boasts the most.

A misfit at heart, he's the fun kind of dread,
While tickling turtles, he rises instead.
His jaws may be fierce, but the jest is real,
Making friends with the crabs who juggle a meal.

Underneath the ripples, a court jester reigns,
Joking with jellyfish, exchanging terrain.
A quick little chase only to tease,
With his laughter, the ocean feels like a breeze.

With a flick of his tail, he swirls and he spins,
While the echoes of chuckles come from within.
In this watery realm where mischief unfolds,
Silly jarring images, the best of the molds.

## Shadows in the Blue

In twilight waters, misfits convene,
With a wave and a wink, so humorous and keen.
Beneath shimmery shades, they play hide and seek,
While seahorses giggle and dolphins peek.

A ruckus awakens, the laughter grows loud,
As they whirl through the eddies, a wiggly crowd.
No need for fright in the dim twilight,
Just fun-loving friends who delight in the night.

With a flip and a flop, they move side to side,
Creating chaos where shadows abide.
Jokingly hungry, they're all in a row,
But sushi and snacks aren't the aim of the show.

As beams of the moonlight dance on the tide,
They frolic in mischief, mischief their guide.
In the shadows of blue, laughter cascades,
With the ocean's soft hum spinning vibrant parades.

## **Communion in the Shadows**

In murky depths they plot and scheme,
A finned committee, living the dream.
They gather 'round a coral table,
Holding court like a tall tale fable.

With wiggly worms as their delegate,
Discussing the price of kelp at a rate.
A light-hearted feast, they munch and dine,
Laughing at fish who think they're divine.

Like underwater gossip, tales unfold,
Of funny fish stories that never get old.
With winks and jests, they splash and play,
In a comedy club where seaweed holds sway.

And as the ocean laughs in waves of glee,
They sign off each meeting with a splashy decree.
For shadows thrive in the whimsical sea,
Where the punchlines flow from their gills, free as can be.

## Twilight's Silent Predation

As daylight wanes, they plot with flair,
Decked in sequins, a fishy affair.
They take to the water without any fright,
Dancing in silence, ready to bite.

Beneath the surface, a rock and roll band,
Playing drum beats with a fin-like hand.
With every wiggle, they steal the show,
Joking at jellies that sail to and fro.

Their favorite snack? A delicacy fine,
Getting laughed at by dolphins, oh divine!
But in twilight's grace, they charge with a grin,
Making each hunt a hilarious win.

So when the shadows begin to sing,
Remember the laughter that the night can bring.
For in this ballet, with gills so grand,
Twilight swims by with a comedic hand.

## Guardians of the Twilight Blue

In the twilight blue, they stand on guard,
Sixteen eyes wide, but not very hard.
Just a bunch of pals, in the deep, they dwell,
Trading off tales, sharing a laugh swell.

With fins flapping wildly, they master the tease,
Casting shadows with such charming ease.
A game of tag in the shimmering tide,
Racing through currents, with pride as their guide.

They protect their domain in ridiculous ways,
Cracking up crabs with their snappy displays.
With laughter echoing, they draw in the night,
Guardians of humor, glow-in-the-dark delight.

A spectacle of joy, in this liquid ball,
Monsters with smiles, the best from us all.
And as the moon rises, the stage is set,
For the guardians of blue, never a threat.

## Choreographed Predation

With a splash and a dive, they begin the show,
Underwater dancers, putting on flow.
A ballet of fins, in a silent trance,
Swift bodies twirling in a graceful dance.

Each move is lively, absurdly grand,
A waltz with the waves, it's all unplanned.
They sneak up on snacks with a pirouette,
And giggle at fish, trapped in their fret.

From the coral stage, the audience sways,
Cheering for the folly of their watery ways.
With a flick of a tail and a wink of an eye,
They claim the night, as the tides whisper by.

In this frolicsome world, where laughter's the key,
They perform their craft, so ceaselessly free.
Choreographed chaos, brimming with glee,
All in the name of a hefty fish spree.

## Masters of the Liquid Domain

In the depths they quietly roam,
Fins waving like they're at home.
Curious glances, a toothy grin,
Who knew the fun would begin?

With a splash and a playful twirl,
They dance through the bubbles that swirl.
Fish scatter, but all in good cheer,
'It's a game!' they say with a sneer.

Undersea antics, a circus of glee,
Chasing tails, oh what a sight to see!
Tuxedoed in style, they strike a fine pose,
Masters of mischief, in tails they do those!

So they glide with a jig and a laugh,
Making waves, oh, what a path!
In this watery realm, they rule the terrain,
Who knew the deep could be such a game?

## Shadows that Drift

Like shadows in a midnight show,
They glide along, moving slow.
With a wink and a toothy grin,
They whisper, 'Let the games begin!'

Beneath the waves, they like to tease,
Silly dances that aim to please.
A little flip, a gentle swoop,
Turns the ocean into a loop!

Oh, what's that lurking, don't be scared,
It's just a joke, not a dare!
With a goofy grin, they swim about,
Creating chaos, without a doubt!

In waters dark, there's always fun,
Bubbles burst and laughter's spun.
With each dive and playful chase,
Life in the deep is a joyful race!

## Anonymity of the Deep

In murky depths where secrets hide,
They glide around, filled with pride.
A joke or jibe in every swell,
Unseen jesters weave their spell!

With stealthy moves and silent laughs,
They plan their pranks and playful shafts.
A tickle here, a nibble there,
Making ripples, raising flair!

Behind the rocks, they chuckle low,
The splash of fun, a bubbling show.
Unseen comedians of the ocean floor,
Bristling with giggles, they always want more.

As shadows sway and mirrors twist,
They dance with joy, no chance of a mist.
In the deep where mystery reigns,
They're the kings of comedy in flowing lanes!

## Lurkers of the Blue Expanse

In the blue expanse, they snoop and sneak,
With flippered feet, it's adventure they seek.
Playful predators in a masks of disguise,
Sneaking surprise with twinkling eyes!

Pausing mid-swim to pull a prank,
Flipping up, making fish tanks!
"Gotcha!" they cry, a laugh in the tide,
Creating giggles where secrets abide.

These clever lurkers, kings of the sea,
Play peek-a-boo with glee!
Every corner hides a jest,
In this aquatic carnival, they are the guest!

With a swirl and a giggle, they chase away gloom,
Creating a bubble of joyous room.
In the vast ocean where laughter's the cast,
The fun-loving lurkers, are a hoot, unsurpassed!

## Echoes of the Silent Chase

In the depths where flippers glide,
Noodles swim, with fish as guides.
A sneaky grin, a toothy yawn,
That big guy's planning a lawn-dart dawn.

A flick of tail, they prance and play,
Doing the cha-cha in a wavy ballet.
With belly laughs, they twirl and sway,
Oh, for a snack, the jokes they will weigh.

In a whirlpool of giggles and grace,
They hide behind rocks, just in case.
Jaws open wide, a toothy surprise,
Laughter erupts, to our sheer surprise!

So hold onto your fins, don't drift too far,
These jester fish are quite bizarre.
With a splash and dash, they make a mark,
Diving in laughter, they leave a spark.

## Ghosts of the Tidal Rage

From the waves emerge strange sights,
Floating pranks on stormy nights.
A jellyfish wearing a top hat, how grand!
Join the seabed's dance, it's all quite planned.

They nibble on foam and frolic in the spray,
Ghostly giggles lead seas away.
With a wink and a twist, they dart with glee,
Leaving bubbles and chuckles, oh, can't you see?

Whispers of fun echo in the swell,
As fish-tales weave their undersea spell.
A party of ghouls, they dance on sand,
Popcorn seashells, a crunchy band!

So beware of the fun in the deep and dark,
They pull pranks on whales, leaving their mark.
With tentacles waving, they bubble and sway—
These tidal ghosts turn night into play!

## Veiled Majesty of the Sea

In the kingdom beneath the gleam,
Monarch fish plot their playful scheme.
With crowns of seaweed, they strut around,
Throwing a ball on the vibrant ground.

While clams play drums, and snails hum tunes,
They spark a dance under glowing moons.
A regal wave, a flip, a twist,
When laughter echoes, who'd dare resist?

With shimmering scales like royal attire,
They boldly tackle the sea's wild choir.
In every ripple, a joke's to be found,
As they caper and cut up, acrobats abound.

So salute the rulers in this watery maze,
Where yuletide vibes create a craze.
For in the deep, where silence can be,
Majesty lives in rippling spree!

## Secrets in the Dark Waters

Down below where the sunlight fades,
Creepy legends swim in sea glades.
Giggles bubble from the clams' tight lips,
But they're only secrets, just playful quips.

Under the cover of mystery vast,
Swirling shadows, they're having a blast.
With sea cucumbers as comedic stars,
They reenact life, giving it a spar.

A dolphin grin, a wink of an eye,
Tickles and giggles in the ocean sky.
With plankton confetti, they celebrate,
The winking sea's joy as they gyrate.

So dive to the depths of giggling tides,
Unravel the mysteries where humor abides.
In every shadow, a tale can spark,
Just smile with the waves, dance in the dark!

## Submerged Monoliths

In the deep where giggles burst,
Monsters dance, not quite rehearsed,
Flippers flap, a silly sight,
Turning gloom to sheer delight.

Bubbles rise, their laughter loud,
Unseen jokes beneath the cloud,
They twirl and glide with clownish flair,
Masters of the water's air.

Their teeth inflate, and grin so wide,
Swirling tricks they cannot hide,
A party held in ocean's core,
Where goofy creatures always score.

With giddy flips, they mock the tide,
No need for fear, just playful pride,
They may be scary, but be advised,
These shadows wear a silly guise.

## **Predatory Grace**

Gliding sleek, with quite a show,
Dressed in scales, but never slow,
With a wink and a daring leap,
They make the clowns, well, laugh and weep.

With open jaws, they strike a pose,
In the current, giggles flow,
Each sharp tooth, a toothy grin,
A vaudeville act that draws you in.

Beneath the waves, a dance of fate,
With fins that twist and twist, they rate,
They prance and play in ocean's lights,
Crowning moments, funny sights.

Adventurous spirits, they embrace,
With playful bounds that set the pace,
Not fierce, but with a flair divine,
These lords of laughter reign in brine.

## Midnight's Fabric

In the night where whispers glide,
Fin-tipped phantoms take their ride,
Draped in moonlight's silken sheen,
  They're the jesters, never mean.

Foamy bubbles burst in cheer,
Chasing giggles that disappear,
A carnival beneath the waves,
Hilarious antics in ocean caves.

Mimicking shadows, they do a jig,
With winks and wiggles, oh so big,
They play tag 'neath a starry cloak,
Delighted minds in laughter soak.

So if you hear a silly sound,
Know that fun is all around,
In the marine masquerade,
Joyful pranks are always made.

## Beneath the Surface Tension

Underneath the worry's crest,
Jovial creatures take their quest,
With sharky smiles and playful schemes,
They craft their laughter out of dreams.

Swirling frights, they slip and slide,
Under waves where giggles ride,
With an air of calm, they tease and jest,
As silly fins outshine the rest.

When currents twist in a goofy dance,
They turn the tide; a comic chance,
Paddling soft, with cheeky grace,
They rule the depths, each fun-filled space.

So roam the ocean, hold not your breath,
For laughter reigns beyond all depth,
In shadows deep, there's no tension,
Only glee in their vast dimension.

## Beneath the Silver Wave

In the depths where fish play hide and seek,
Chompers grin, their smiles rather bleak.
With fins like torpedoes, they dash and dive,
Cracking jokes that make the seaweed thrive.

With bubble-blowing antics and a flip,
They twirl with glee, giving each fish a skip.
Gulping down snacks, they munch with delight,
A feast of giggles in the moon's soft light.

While dolphins laugh with their splashy flair,
The glimmers below are treated with care.
Oh, those toothy jesters with a wink and a grin,
Make every sea critter think twice before diving in!

But hey, what's that? It's a game of tag!
Oh, splish-splash, they missed like a wag!
Underneath the waves, it's a comedy scene,
Where the tales of the ocean are quite the routine!

## Ghosts of the Deep

In the ink-black water, with a whoosh and a swish,
Float eerie forms, not one is a fish.
They glide and they laugh, giving quite a scare,
But underneath those frights, it's just a fish fair!

With jelly-like bodies and eyes so round,
They tickle the seafloor without making a sound.
Casting shadows, they dance in the night,
While the clueless crabs scuttle in fright.

Oh, what a sight when they swarm on by,
With wriggly tentacles, they reach for the sky.
They whisper soft jokes to startled old eels,
While the octopuses chuckle behind their meals.

So don't be alarmed by the eerie white glow,
It's just a fun party where mischief does flow.
Ghosts of the sea, with their playful ballet,
Bring laughter and sport to the deep's grand display!

## Predators of the Twilight

When twilight descends, they emerge with flair,
The kings of the deep with a mischievous stare.
Swapping fish stories as they jostle for eats,
They're the clowns of the ocean in their colorful fleets.

With wide-open mouths and an appetite keen,
They try to catch snacks, but it's all just a scene.
A flurry of fins, a splish and a thud,
Leaving poor sardines in a giggly flood.

Their chompers shine bright like the stars above,
Searching for treats in the waters they love.
Each nibble's a joke in a feast that's surreal,
While the clownfish all chuckle, enjoying the meal.

As creatures of night flaunt their spooky charm,
These wacky munchers bring everyone harm.
But fret not, dear swimmer, just swim with delight,
For the true jesters of night are a comical sight!

## Silent Hunters of the Abyss

In darkness they move, with all stealth and grace,
Crafty swimmers with a whimsical face.
They stalk through the night, but it's all for the tease,
Chasing those fish with the greatest of ease.

But don't you think twice as they glide without sound,
Those fins are for laughter, not to fear on the ground.
A game of hide-and-seek, they play with such flair,
While the plankton dance gaily in the cool ocean air.

With a splash and a giggle, they swish their long tails,
Creating a ripple far deeper than tales.
Every nibble's a joke and each spin's just for fun,
Making waves in the abyss, until the day is done.

So, next time you glimpse that shadowy guise,
Remember they're jesters with laughter in their eyes.
At the edge of the blue, where the gaggles all play,
It's a circus that thrives, come and join in the fray!

www.ingramcontent.com/pod-product-compliance
Lightning Source LLC
Chambersburg PA
CBHW060111230426
43661CB00003B/152